ABOUT T...

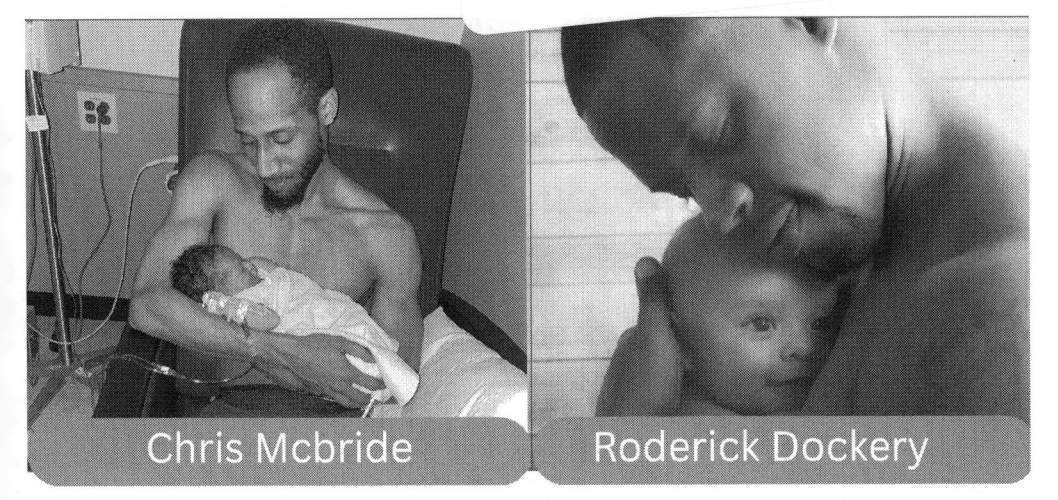

Chris Mcbride

Roderick Dockery

AS TWO MEN WHO WERE RAISED BY SINGLE MOTHERS WITHOUT THE PRESENCE OF A FATHER, WE KNOW FIRSTHAND THE CHALLENGES THAT COME WITH FATHERLESSNESS. WE UNDERSTAND THE IMPACT THAT IT CAN HAVE ON A YOUNG BOY'S LIFE AND THE DIFFICULTIES THAT FATHERS WHO ARE RAISING SONS ON THEIR OWN CAN FACE.

HOWEVER, WE ALSO KNOW THAT WITH THE RIGHT GUIDANCE, SUPPORT, AND MINDSET, IT'S POSSIBLE TO OVERCOME THESE CHALLENGES AND RAISE STRONG, CONFIDENT, AND RESILIENT YOUNG MEN.

THAT'S WHY WE'VE CREATED "DAD BY CHOICE: OVERCOMING FATHERLESSNESS, REDEFINING FATHERHOOD, & BUILDING A LASTING LEGACY." THIS BOOK IS DESIGNED TO EMPOWER FATHERLESS FATHERS WITH THE KNOWLEDGE, TOOLS, AND RESOURCES THEY NEED TO NAVIGATE THE COMPLEXITIES OF RAISING SONS ON THEIR OWN.

WE KNOW THAT BEING A SINGLE FATHER CAN BE OVERWHELMING AT TIMES, BUT WE WANT TO ENCOURAGE YOU THAT YOU ARE NOT ALONE. WITH OUR BOOK, YOU WILL GAIN INSIGHTS AND PRACTICAL ADVICE THAT WILL HELP YOU BUILD A STRONG RELATIONSHIP WITH YOUR SON, DEVELOP HIS CONFIDENCE, AND GUIDE HIM ON HIS JOURNEY TO BECOMING A SUCCESSFUL AND FULFILLED MAN.

WE ALSO WANT TO HIGHLIGHT THE IMPORTANCE OF STRONG MEN IN THE LIVES OF BOYS. AS FATHERLESS FATHERS, YOU HAVE A UNIQUE OPPORTUNITY TO BE THE POSITIVE MALE INFLUENCE THAT YOUR SON NEEDS. YOUR PRESENCE, GUIDANCE, AND LOVE CAN MAKE ALL THE DIFFERENCE IN HIS LIFE AND SHAPE HIM INTO THE BEST VERSION OF HIMSELF.

WE BELIEVE THAT EVERY FATHERLESS FATHER HAS THE POTENTIAL TO BE A GREAT DAD AND RAISE EXCEPTIONAL YOUNG MEN. WE HOPE THAT OUR BOOK WILL INSPIRE AND EMPOWER YOU ON YOUR JOURNEY, PROVIDING YOU WITH THE CONFIDENCE AND SUPPORT YOU NEED TO EMBRACE FATHERHOOD AND RAISE YOUR SON TO HIS FULLEST POTENTIAL.

OLIVIA WILSON   WORKBOOK

TABLE OF CONTENTS

Foreword
- The author's personal experience as a fatherless father
- The mission to help fatherless fathers break the cycle

01 Introduction
- The impact of fatherlessness on children, families, and communities
- The purpose and goals of the book

02 Building Strong Relationships with Your Children
- The importance of father-child bonding
- Effective communication strategies
- Developing emotional intelligence and empathy
- Establishing routines and rituals
- Navigating challenges in father-child relationships

03 Fostering a Healthy Marriage or Partnership
- The role of a father in a healthy relationship
- Balancing fatherhood and partnership responsibilities
- Communication and conflict resolution skills
- Fostering intimacy and emotional connection
- Supporting your partner in their parenting journey

04 Healing from the Trauma of Fatherlessness
- Identifying and acknowledging the effects of fatherlessness
- Strategies for healing and personal growth
- Building a support network
- The role of therapy and professional help
- Forgiveness and letting go of the past

TABLE OF CONTENTS

05 Personal Growth and Becoming the Man You Were Meant to Be
- Identifying and developing personal values and beliefs
- Developing self-awareness and emotional intelligence
- Setting and achieving personal and professional goals
- Embracing vulnerability and authenticity
- Building resilience and adapting to change

06 Learning from Experts and Other Fatherless Fathers
- The benefits of expert insights and experiences
- Understanding different perspectives on fatherlessness
- Networking and building connections within the fatherless fathers community
- Applying lessons learned to your own fatherhood journey

07 Being a Role Model for Your Children and Future Generations
- The importance of being a positive role model
- Instilling values and principles in your children
- Encouraging and supporting your children's dreams and aspirations
- Promoting healthy relationships and communication within the family
- Leaving a legacy for future generations

08 Conclusion
- Reflecting on personal growth and progress
- Identifying areas for continued growth and development
- Setting future goals as a father, husband, and individual
- Staying connected with the fatherless fathers community
- Embracing the imperfect father's journey and striving for growth and improvement

TABLE OF CONTENTS

09 Appendix

- Additional resources for fatherless fathers
- Recommended books, podcasts, and organizations
- Support groups and online communities

Chapter #1 Building Strong Relationships with Your Children

DAD BY CHOICE:
Overcoming Fatherlessness, Redefining Fatherhood & Building a Lasting Legacy

"A good father is one of the most unsung, unpraised, unnoticed, and yet one of the most valuable assets in our society." - Billy Graham

Chapter 1: The Far-Reaching Effects of Fatherlessness and How to Rise Above Them

Impactful facts about fatherless fathers:

According to the U.S. Census Bureau, 1 in 4 children in the United States live without a father in the home. This fact highlights the prevalence of fatherlessness and the potential impact it can have on children and families.

Fatherlessness can have negative effects on a child's development, including increased risk of poverty, academic difficulties, and behavioral problems. This fact emphasizes the potential consequences of fatherlessness and underscores the importance of fathers in a child's life.

Research has shown that fatherless fathers are more likely to struggle with mental health issues such as depression and anxiety. This fact highlights the personal struggles that fatherless fathers may face as a result of their own fatherlessness.

Fatherless fathers may have difficulty forming healthy relationships with other men, including father figures or mentors. This fact underscores the potential long-term impact of fatherlessness on a person's ability to form relationships and connect with others.

Fatherless fathers may have a more difficult time developing a sense of self-worth or confidence. This fact highlights the potential psychological consequences of growing up without a father, which can affect a person's self-perception and overall well-being.

Fatherlessness: The Invisible Epidemic

As you sit down to read this book, take a moment to consider this startling fact: millions of children worldwide grow up without a father figure in their lives. Whether due to abandonment, divorce, death, or any other circumstance, the absence of a father has a profound impact on these children and their families. Fatherlessness is an invisible epidemic that doesn't discriminate; it affects people from all walks of life, transcending cultural, racial, and economic boundaries.

But let's not dwell on the gloom and doom. Instead, let's take a closer look at the far-reaching consequences of fatherlessness and explore practical strategies for overcoming these challenges. Together, we'll discover how to turn our personal pain into a powerful force for positive change. And who knows? We might even have a few laughs along the way.

Chapter 1: The Far-Reaching Effects of Fatherlessness and How to Rise Above Them

The Domino Effect: Mental Health, Emotional Well-Being, and Economic Stability

The effects of fatherlessness are like a set of dominoes, each piece toppling the next, creating a cascade of challenges that impact mental health, emotional well-being, and even economic stability. Let's take a closer look at this domino effect and how it plays out in the lives of children and families affected by fatherlessness.

Mental Health: Children growing up without a father figure are at a higher risk for depression, anxiety, and other mental health issues. Like a bicycle without training wheels, these children often feel unsteady and unsupported, navigating the bumpy road of life without a guiding hand. This emotional instability can lead to a host of mental health problems, including substance abuse and even suicidal thoughts.

Emotional Well-Being: Fatherlessness can also have a significant impact on a child's emotional well-being. Children without a father figure may struggle with feelings of abandonment, resentment, and low self-esteem. They might wonder, "Why wasn't my dad around? Was it something I did? Am I not good enough?" These negative emotions can create a heavy burden for children to carry, affecting their relationships and overall quality of life.

Economic Stability: Finally, let's not forget the financial implications of fatherlessness. Single-parent households often face economic hardships due to the loss of a breadwinner. These financial struggles can lead to a cycle of poverty that can be difficult to break, perpetuating the cycle of fatherlessness for future generations.

Now that we've painted a somewhat grim picture of the consequences of fatherlessness, let's pivot to something more hopeful. Let's talk about the practical strategies we can use to overcome these challenges and create a brighter future for ourselves and our families.

Chapter 1: The Far-Reaching Effects of Fatherlessness and How to Rise Above Them

Practical Strategies for Overcoming the Effects of Fatherlessness

Imagine you're at the bottom of a mountain, staring up at the peak, wondering how on earth you'll ever reach the top. It's a daunting task, no doubt, but with the right tools and guidance, it's entirely possible to conquer the mountain of fatherlessness. Here are some strategies to help you start your ascent:

Acknowledge the Impact: The first step in overcoming fatherlessness is acknowledging the impact it has had on your life. This might seem like a no-brainer, but it's crucial to confront the pain and disappointment of growing up without a father figure. It's like ripping off a Band-Aid: it might sting at first, but it's necessary for healing. By recognizing the influence of fatherlessness on your mental health, emotional well-being, and economic stability, you can begin to take control of your future.

Seek Professional Help: Therapy and counseling can be invaluable resources for those affected by fatherlessness. A trained professional can help you process your feelings, develop coping strategies, and provide guidance on your journey to healing. Don't be afraid to reach out for help; sometimes, talking to an unbiased expert can be just the ticket to gaining clarity and understanding.

Build a Support Network: Surround yourself with friends, family, and mentors who can offer encouragement, advice, and a listening ear. Building a strong support network is like constructing a safety net that can catch you when you fall and help you bounce back from setbacks. It's also essential to connect with others who have experienced fatherlessness; their insights and shared experiences can be a source of comfort and inspiration.

Chapter 1: The Far-Reaching Effects of Fatherlessness and How to Rise Above Them

Focus on Personal Growth: Invest time and energy in developing yourself, both as an individual and as a parent. Engage in activities that promote self-awareness, emotional intelligence, and resilience. This might include reading self-help books, attending workshops, or practicing mindfulness and meditation. By focusing on personal growth, you can cultivate the qualities needed to become the best version of yourself, rising above the challenges of fatherlessness.

Strengthen Relationships: Take active steps to strengthen your relationships with your children, partner, and others in your life. Make time for bonding activities, improve your communication skills, and practice empathy and understanding. By nurturing these relationships, you can create a stable, loving environment that promotes emotional well-being for everyone involved.

Break the Cycle: Embrace your role as a father and commit to being the supportive, loving parent that you never had. By doing so, you can break the cycle of fatherlessness and create a brighter future for your children and future generations. Remember, it's not about being perfect; it's about being present, engaged, and committed to being the best father you can be.

Find Humor and Inspiration: Throughout your journey, don't forget to find humor and inspiration in your experiences. Laughter can be a powerful coping mechanism, helping you to navigate difficult emotions and maintain perspective. Additionally, seek out stories of others who have overcome fatherlessness, using their triumphs as motivation to continue your own journey.

Chapter 1: The Far-Reaching Effects of Fatherlessness and How to Rise Above Them

Climbing the Mountain: Embracing Your Journey as a Dad

As you embark on your journey to overcome the effects of fatherlessness, remember that you're not alone. Millions of others have faced similar challenges and come out on the other side, stronger and more resilient. Like climbing a mountain, the path may be steep and treacherous, but with determination, support, and the right strategies, you can reach the summit.

So, strap on your metaphorical hiking boots and get ready to embrace your journey as a dad. Along the way, you'll find moments of joy, pain, laughter, and profound insight. And when you finally reach the top of that mountain, you'll look back on your journey with a sense of accomplishment, knowing that you've conquered fatherlessness and become the loving, supportive parent your children deserve.

Chapter 1: The Far-Reaching Effects of Fatherlessness and How to Rise Above Them

As you close this chapter and continue reading, keep in mind that overcoming fatherlessness is not a one-size-fits-all journey. Your path may be different from someone else's, but the essential thing is that you're moving forward, making progress, and growing as a person and a parent.

With a healthy dose of wit, humor, and determination, you're now equipped to tackle fatherlessness head-on and rise above its challenges. So, let's continue this journey together, exploring practical strategies for strengthening relationships, fostering personal growth, and ultimately, becoming the best version of ourselves as fathers and partners.

"Fatherhood has given me a sense of purpose and a reason to keep pushing forward. I want to be the best father I can be for my children." Nipsey Hussle

Name: _____   Date: _____

Chapter 1 Quiz

Lets see what you learned in chapter #1

1. Fatherlessness is an _____ epidemic that affects millions of children worldwide.

   _____

2. The effects of fatherlessness create a _____ effect on mental health, emotional well-being, and economic stability.

   _____

3. Therapy and counseling can be _____ resources for those affected by fatherlessness.

   _____

4. By focusing on _____ growth, you can cultivate the qualities needed to become the best version of yourself

   _____

5. What is the first step in overcoming fatherlessness?
    a. Ignore the impact
    b. Acknowledge the impact
    c. Seek professional help
    5.d. Build a support network

6. Which of the following is NOT a practical strategy for overcoming the effects of fatherlessness?
    a. Strengthen relationships
    b. Avoid talking about the issue
    c. Focus on personal growth
    d. Break the cycle

Name: _____   Date: _____

Chapter 1 Quiz
Lets see what you learned in chapter #1

7. What is essential when building a support network?
   a. Connecting with others who have experienced fatherlessness
   b. Isolating yourself from others
   c. Ignoring the problem
   d. None of the above

Journaling Prompt

Reflect on your own experience with fatherlessness or the absence of a father figure. Write a paragraph describing the challenges you faced and how they affected your mental health, emotional well-being, and economic stability. Consider the practical strategies mentioned in the chapter and how you can apply them to your own life to rise above the challenges of fatherlessness.

Chapter #2 Forging Unbreakable Bonds Building Strong Relationships with Your Children

"Any man can be a father, but it takes someone special to be a dad."

Chapter 2: Fostering a Healthy Marriage or Partnership

The Crucial Connection

If you've ever watched a nature documentary, you've likely seen footage of a newborn animal taking its first wobbly steps, instinctively following its parent. It's a touching sight, isn't it? This powerful bond between parent and child is not only heartwarming but also essential for the offspring's survival and development.

Just like those newborn animals, your children need a strong connection with you to thrive. As a father, building and maintaining a robust and loving relationship with your children is crucial for their emotional, mental, and social well-being. In this chapter, we'll explore the importance of father-child bonding and provide practical tips to strengthen these connections. So, buckle up and get ready for a roller coaster ride through the highs and lows of parenting – one that's sure to be filled with laughter, tears, and a whole lot of love.

Section 1: The Power of Communication: Strategies for Fathers and Children

You've probably heard the saying, "communication is key." It might sound like a cliché, but when it comes to building strong relationships with your children, it's absolutely true. In this section, we'll dive into effective communication strategies for fathers and children that will help you create lasting connections.

"Any man can be a father, but it takes someone special to be a dad."

Chapter 2: Fostering a Healthy Marriage or Partnership

Active Listening: The first step in effective communication is active listening. This means truly hearing what your child is saying, without interrupting or jumping to conclusions. By being an attentive listener, you show your child that you value their thoughts and feelings, which in turn helps to build trust and strengthen your bond.

Open-Ended Questions: Encourage open and honest communication with your child by asking open-ended questions that invite them to share their thoughts and feelings. Instead of asking, "Did you have a good day at school?" try, "What was the best part of your day?" This approach encourages your child to open up and share more about their experiences, fostering a deeper connection between the two of you.

Be Approachable: Make sure your child knows they can come to you with any issue or concern, no matter how big or small. Create an environment where your child feels comfortable talking to you about anything, without fear of judgment or criticism. By being approachable and receptive, you're laying the foundation for a strong and trusting relationship.

Express Your Feelings: As a father, it's essential to model healthy communication by expressing your feelings openly and honestly. Share your joys, fears, and frustrations with your child, and let them see that it's okay to express emotions. In doing so, you're teaching your child valuable emotional skills and fostering a deeper connection.

Chapter 2: Fostering a Healthy Marriage or Partnership

Emotional Intelligence and Empathy: Understanding Your Child's World

If communication is the foundation of a strong father-child relationship, emotional intelligence and empathy are the bricks and mortar that hold it together. In this section, we'll explore the importance of developing these skills and how they can strengthen your bond with your child.

Recognize and Validate Emotions: Teach your child to identify and express their emotions by acknowledging and validating their feelings. For example, if your child is upset because they didn't make the soccer team, say, "I understand that you're disappointed, and it's okay to feel that way." By recognizing and validating their emotions, you're helping your child develop emotional intelligence and creating a safe space for them to share their feelings.

Practice Empathy: Put yourself in your child's shoes and try to see the world from their perspective. Empathy is the ability to understand and share the feelings of another, and it's a crucial skill for building strong relationships. By practicing empathy, you can better understand your child's emotions and experiences, allowing you to provide the support and guidance they need.

Encourage Emotional Expression: Create an environment where your child feels comfortable expressing their emotions. Encourage them to share their feelings, whether it's through talking, writing, drawing, or other creative outlets. This not only helps your child develop emotional intelligence but also strengthens your bond as they feel understood and supported.

Chapter 2: Fostering a Healthy Marriage or Partnership

Routines and Rituals: Creating Opportunities for Connection

Just as a house needs a solid foundation and sturdy walls, your relationship with your child requires regular maintenance to stay strong. Establishing routines and rituals can help you create consistent opportunities for connection and bonding. In this section, we'll explore some ideas for building these meaningful moments into your daily life.

Bedtime Routine: Establish a consistent bedtime routine that includes quality time with your child. This might involve reading a story, talking about their day, or simply cuddling. A nightly ritual like this can help your child feel secure and loved, strengthening your bond.

Family Meals: Make an effort to have regular family meals, where everyone sits down to eat and chat together. This provides a perfect opportunity for open communication and bonding, creating a sense of togetherness and belonging.

Special Outings: Plan regular outings or activities that are just for you and your child, like a weekly bike ride, movie night, or trip to the park. These special moments help create lasting memories and deepen your connection.

Celebrate Achievements: Acknowledge and celebrate your child's achievements, both big and small. This could be as simple as praising a good grade or attending their school performance. By showing your support and encouragement, you're reinforcing your bond and helping to build their self-esteem.

Chapter 2: Fostering a Healthy Marriage or Partnership

Address Conflict Constructively: When conflict arises, address it head-on, but do so with respect and empathy. Use "I" statements to express your feelings and thoughts, and avoid blaming or criticizing your child. By handling conflict constructively, you're teaching your child valuable life skills and maintaining a strong connection.

Be Patient and Persistent: Building a strong relationship with your child takes time and effort. Be patient with the process and persistent in your efforts to connect, even when it's difficult. Remember, Rome wasn't built in a day, and neither is a strong father-child bond.

Adapt and Evolve: As your child grows and changes, so too must your relationship. Be willing to adapt and evolve to meet your child's changing needs, interests, and personality. This flexibility will help you maintain a strong connection through all stages of their life.

Seek Help When Needed: If you're struggling to connect with your child or facing significant challenges in your relationship, don't hesitate to seek help from a therapist or counselor. These professionals can offer guidance, support, and strategies for strengthening your bond.

Chapter 2: Fostering a Healthy Marriage or Partnership

The Journey of a Lifetime

Building strong relationships with your children is not a destination, but rather a journey – one filled with laughter, tears, and countless learning opportunities. By embracing effective communication, developing emotional intelligence and empathy, establishing routines and rituals, and navigating challenges with grace and perseverance, you're well on your way to forging unbreakable bonds with your children.

As you continue to read and explore the strategies outlined in this chapter, remember that every family is unique, and there's no one-size-fits-all approach to parenting. Trust your instincts, lean on your support network, and be open to learning and growing as a father. In doing so, you'll not only build strong relationships with your children but also set a powerful example of love, resilience, and growth that they'll carry with them throughout their lives.

So, take a deep breath, pat yourself on the back, and continue on this incredible journey of fatherhood. Together, you and your children will navigate the twists and turns, conquer the challenges, and create a lifetime of precious memories. And remember, it's not about being perfect; it's about being present, engaged, and committed to being the best father you can be – for them, for you, and for generations to come.

"As a father, it's important to me to be a role model for my children. I want them to see me as someone they can look up to and respect." Jay Z

Name: _____ Date: _____

Chapter 2 Quiz
Lets see what you learned in chapter #2

1. 1.Building and maintaining a _____ and _____ relationship with your children is crucial for their emotional, mental, and social well-being.

2. Active _____ is the first step in effective communication with your child.

3. Emotional _____ and _____ are essential skills for building strong relationships with your children.

4. Establishing _____ and _____ can help create consistent opportunities for connection and bonding.

5. Which of the following is an example of an open-ended question?
   a. Did you have a good day at school?
   b. What was the best part of your day?
   c. Are you okay?

6. To practice empathy, you should:
   a. Ignore your child's emotions
   b. Put yourself in your child's shoes and try to see the world from their perspective
   c. Only focus on your own emotions

Name: _____   Date: _____

Chapter 2 Quiz
Lets see what you learned in chapter #2

7. A consistent bedtime routine can help your child feel:
   a. Anxious
   b. Secure and loved
   c. Overwhelmed

   _____

8. When navigating challenges in your relationship with your child, it's important to:
   a. Address conflict constructively
   b. Be impatient
   c. Avoid discussing difficult topics

   _____

   Journaling Prompt:
   Reflect on your current relationship with your child(ren). Identify one area where you'd like to improve your connection and describe the steps you plan to take in order to strengthen that bond.

   _____

Chapter #3 Fostering a Healthy Marriage or partnership

"Fatherhood is not about being perfect, it's about being present. You have to be there for your children, no matter what." Myles Munroe

Chapter 3: *Fostering a Healthy Marriage or partnership*

The Dynamic Duo

Picture your favorite superhero duo – Batman and Robin, perhaps? Or maybe it's Captain America and Bucky Barnes? What makes these duos so powerful is not only their individual strengths but also the way they work together as a team. When faced with a challenge, they combine their talents, rely on each other's support, and ultimately emerge victorious.

Now, let's bring this metaphor into your world. As a father, you and your partner are your own superhero duo, working together to navigate the challenges of parenting and build a strong, loving family. A healthy partnership is essential for both you and your children, providing a solid foundation for emotional well-being and growth. In this chapter, we'll discuss strategies for cultivating a loving and supportive relationship with your partner while balancing the responsibilities of fatherhood. So, grab your cape and let's dive in!

The Role of a Father in a Healthy Relationship

You've probably heard the saying, "happy wife, happy life" or, in more inclusive terms, "happy spouse, happy house." While it may be a bit of an oversimplification, there's a kernel of truth in the sentiment. A strong and healthy partnership benefits not only you and your partner but also your children. In this section, we'll explore the role of a father in a healthy relationship.

Chapter 3: Fostering a Healthy Marriage or partnership

Emotional Support: As a father and partner, one of your most crucial roles is to provide emotional support for your partner. This means being there to listen, empathize, and offer a shoulder to lean on during both the good times and the bad.

Shared Responsibilities: In a healthy relationship, both partners share the responsibilities of parenting and household tasks. This includes everything from diaper changes and bedtime routines to grocery shopping and meal preparation. By working together as a team, you can lighten the load for each other and create a more harmonious home environment.

Open Communication: Keep the lines of communication open with your partner, discussing your thoughts, feelings, and concerns openly and honestly. By maintaining a strong connection with your partner, you can better navigate the ups and downs of parenting and life in general.

Personal Growth: As a father, it's essential to continue focusing on your personal growth and well-being. This includes nurturing your interests, hobbies, and friendships outside of your relationship and family. A well-rounded and fulfilled individual is better equipped to be a loving and supportive partner and father.

Chapter 3: Fostering a Healthy Marriage or partnership

Balancing Fatherhood and Partnership Responsibilities

Juggling the roles of father and partner can feel like walking a tightrope at times – one misstep, and it feels like everything could come crashing down. Fear not, for in this section, we'll explore strategies for maintaining equilibrium between these two essential roles in your life.

Prioritize Quality Time: Make spending quality time with your partner a priority, even amidst the chaos of parenting. Schedule regular date nights or quiet moments to reconnect, just the two of you. By maintaining your connection as a couple, you'll create a stronger foundation for your family.

Divide and Conquer: Sit down with your partner and discuss the division of parenting and household responsibilities. Work together to create a system that feels fair and balanced, ensuring that both partners feel valued and supported.

Be Flexible: Life is unpredictable, and sometimes you'll need to adapt and adjust your plans to accommodate unforeseen circumstances. Be willing to step in and take on additional responsibilities when needed, and be understanding when your partner needs to do the same.
Make Time for Self-Care: It's essential to carve out time for self-care, both for yourself and your partner.

Encourage each other to pursue hobbies, exercise, or engage in activities that bring joy and relaxation. By taking care of yourselves, you'll be better equipped to support each other and your children.

Chapter 3: Fostering a Healthy Marriage or partnership

Communication and Conflict Resolution Skills

Even in the healthiest of relationships, conflicts are inevitable. The key to maintaining a strong partnership lies in your ability to navigate these conflicts with grace, empathy, and effective communication. In this section, we'll discuss essential skills for resolving disagreements and keeping the lines of communication open with your partner.

Active Listening: When your partner is speaking, give them your full attention. This means putting away distractions, making eye contact, and truly absorbing what they're saying. By actively listening, you're showing your partner that you value their thoughts and feelings.

Use "I" Statements: Express your thoughts and feelings using "I" statements, which focus on your experience rather than placing blame or making accusations. For example, instead of saying, "You never help with the kids," try saying, "I feel overwhelmed when I have to handle all the parenting tasks by myself."

Stay Calm and Respectful: Approach disagreements with a calm and respectful demeanor. Avoid raising your voice, name-calling, or engaging in other aggressive behaviors. By maintaining a respectful tone, you're more likely to have a productive conversation and reach a resolution.

Compromise and Problem-Solve: Work together with your partner to find solutions and compromises that meet both of your needs. This may involve brainstorming ideas, making lists, or even seeking outside help from a therapist or counselor.

Chapter 3: *Fostering a Healthy Marriage or partnership*

Fostering Intimacy and Emotional Connection

A strong emotional connection is the glue that holds your partnership together. In this final section, we'll explore strategies for nurturing intimacy and maintaining a deep emotional bond with your partner.

Express Affection: Show your love and appreciation for your partner through both words and actions. This might include leaving a sweet note, offering a hug or a kiss, or simply saying, "I love you."

Be Vulnerable: Allow yourself to be vulnerable with your partner, sharing your fears, dreams, and insecurities. By opening up to each other, you create a deeper emotional connection and a safe space for mutual support.

Prioritize Emotional Intimacy: Make time for conversations that go beyond the surface level. Ask open-ended questions, share your feelings, and truly listen to your partner's responses. By prioritizing emotional intimacy, you'll build a stronger, more resilient partnership.

Keep the Romance Alive: Remember the early days of your relationship, when everything felt new and exciting? Rekindle that spark by planning romantic outings, surprising your partner with thoughtful gestures, or trying new activities together. By keeping the romance alive, you'll maintain a strong emotional connection and add a little extra zest to your partnership.

Chapter 3: *Fostering a Healthy Marriage or partnership*

A Superhero Duo for the Ages

As we conclude this chapter, remember that cultivating a healthy marriage or partnership is a continuous journey, not a destination. By embracing open communication, shared responsibilities, effective conflict resolution, and emotional intimacy, you'll create a strong, loving bond that benefits both you and your children.

After all, the best gift you can give your children is the example of a healthy, supportive, and loving relationship. So, strap on your superhero cape, grab your partner's hand, and continue on this incredible adventure together – side by side, heart to heart, and stronger than ever.

"Fatherhood is about teaching your children how to think, not what to think. You have to help them develop critical thinking skills." Myles Munroe

Name: _____ Date: _____

Chapter 3 Quiz

Lets see what you learned in chapter #3

1. A father should provide _____ support for their partner

   _____

2. Open _____ is essential to maintaining a strong connection with your partner.

   _____

3. What should be a priority when balancing fatherhood and partnership responsibilities?
   a. Focusing solely on parenting
   B. Prioritizing quality time with your partner
   C. Ignoring self-care
   D. Always putting your needs first
   _____

4. Use "__" Statements to express your thoughts and feelings.

   _____

5. .When your partner is speaking, practice _____ listening.

   _____

6. .Which of the following is NOT a strategy for nurturing intimacy and maintaining a deep emotional bond with your partner?
   A. Expressing affection
   B. Being vulnerable
   C. Avoiding deep conversations
   D. Keeping the romance alive

Name: _____   Date: _____

Chapter 3 Quiz

Lets see what you learned in chapter #3

Journaling Prompt:
Reflect on your relationship with your partner. How do you currently balance fatherhood and partnership responsibilities? What areas could be improved? What steps can you take to enhance communication, intimacy, and emotional connection in your relationship?

List 3 specific actions you can take to foster a healthier relationship with your partner.

1.

2.

3.

Remember, cultivating a healthy marriage or partnership is a continuous journey. By engaging in these workbook activities and embracing open communication, shared responsibilities, effective conflict resolution, and emotional intimacy, you're taking the necessary steps towards building a strong, loving bond that benefits both you and your children. Keep up the good work, and continue on this incredible adventure together – side by side, heart to heart, and stronger than ever!

Chapter # 4 Healing from the Trauma of Fatherlessness

"The greatest gift a father can give his children is his time and attention. They need to know that they are loved and valued." T.D. Jakes

Chapter 4: Healing from the Trauma of Fatherlessness

The Wounds We Carry

Imagine for a moment that you're a skilled gardener, tending to a beautiful, lush garden filled with vibrant flowers and delicious vegetables. You know that in order for your garden to thrive, you must not only nourish and care for the plants but also address any weeds or pests that threaten their health. If left unaddressed, these challenges can undermine the entire garden, diminishing its beauty and vitality.

Now, let's bring this metaphor into the realm of personal growth and healing. As a fatherless father, you carry within you the wounds of fatherlessness – the weeds and pests in your metaphorical garden. In order to heal and grow, you must first identify and acknowledge these wounds, then actively work to address them.

In this chapter, we'll explore strategies for healing from the trauma of fatherlessness, building a support network, and ultimately emerging stronger and more resilient than ever before. So, grab your gardening gloves, and let's get started!

Chapter 4: Healing from the Trauma of Fatherlessness

Identifying and Acknowledging the Effects of Fatherlessness

Before we can heal, we must first understand the wounds we carry. In this section, we'll delve into the various effects of fatherlessness, helping you identify and acknowledge the ways in which it has shaped your life.

Emotional Impact: Fatherlessness can leave an indelible mark on your emotional well-being, leading to feelings of abandonment, insecurity, anger, and sadness. Acknowledging these emotions is the first step in the healing process.

Relationship Patterns: The absence of a father figure can create patterns in your relationships, such as difficulties with trust, intimacy, or communication. Recognizing these patterns can help you begin to address them and cultivate healthier connections with others.

Self-Identity and Self-Worth: Growing up without a father figure can impact your sense of self, leading to feelings of inadequacy or a lack of confidence. By identifying these feelings, you can begin to build a stronger, more secure sense of self.

Coping Mechanisms: In response to the pain of fatherlessness, you may have developed coping mechanisms such as denial, avoidance, or substance use. Understanding these coping strategies can help you identify healthier ways to navigate your emotions and experiences.

Chapter 4: Healing from the Trauma of Fatherlessness

IStrategies for Healing and Personal Growth

Once you've identified and acknowledged the effects of fatherlessness, it's time to begin the process of healing and growth. In this section, we'll explore strategies for nurturing your emotional well-being and cultivating resilience in the face of adversity.

Self-Reflection: Engage in regular self-reflection, whether through journaling, meditation, or other introspective practices. By exploring your thoughts and feelings, you can gain insights into your healing process and personal growth.

Cultivate Self-Compassion: Treat yourself with kindness and understanding, recognizing that healing is a journey filled with ups and downs. Acknowledge your progress and celebrate your successes, no matter how small.

Embrace Vulnerability: Allow yourself to be vulnerable with others, sharing your experiences and emotions openly and honestly. By doing so, you'll build deeper connections and create a support network to help you navigate your healing journey.

Set Boundaries: Establish healthy boundaries in your relationships, ensuring that you prioritize your own well-being and emotional safety. By setting boundaries, you'll create a more balanced and supportive environment for healing and growth.

Chapter 4: Healing from the Trauma of Fatherlessness

Building a Support Network

As the saying goes, "no man is an island." In order to heal and grow, it's essential to surround yourself with a strong support network of friends, family, and professionals who can offer guidance, encouragement, and a listening ear. In this section, we'll discuss strategies for building and maintaining a support network that can help you on your journey of healing and personal growth.

Reach Out: Don't be afraid to reach out to friends, family members, or other trusted individuals in your life. Share your experiences, ask for advice, or simply engage in conversation. By doing so, you'll create connections that can offer support and encouragement during difficult times.

Join a Support Group: Consider joining a support group for fatherless fathers or individuals who have experienced similar challenges. These groups can provide a safe space to share your experiences, learn from others, and build connections with people who understand your journey.

Seek Professional Help: If needed, don't hesitate to seek professional help from therapists, counselors, or coaches who specialize in addressing the effects of fatherlessness. These professionals can offer guidance, resources, and support to help you navigate your healing process.

Cultivate New Friendships: As you grow and heal, it's important to develop new friendships with individuals who share your values and interests. By surrounding yourself with supportive, like-minded people, you'll create a strong foundation for personal growth and happiness.

Chapter 4: Healing from the Trauma of Fatherlessness

The Role of Therapy and Professional Help

While friends and family can offer invaluable support, sometimes professional help is necessary to truly heal from the trauma of fatherlessness. In this section, we'll explore the benefits of therapy and other professional resources.

Unbiased Perspective: Therapists and counselors can offer an unbiased perspective on your experiences, helping you gain new insights and understanding.

Expertise: Professionals who specialize in addressing fatherlessness have a wealth of knowledge and experience to draw upon, providing you with tools and strategies for healing and growth.

Safe Space: Therapy offers a safe and confidential space for you to explore your emotions, experiences, and challenges without fear of judgment or repercussions.

Accountability: Working with a professional can help you stay accountable to your healing journey, ensuring that you continue to make progress and grow.

Chapter 4: Healing from the Trauma of Fatherlessness

Forgiveness and Letting Go of the Past

In order to truly heal from the trauma of fatherlessness, it's essential to forgive and let go of the past. This doesn't mean forgetting or excusing any hurt or harm, but rather releasing the emotional weight of these experiences and moving forward with a newfound sense of freedom and resilience. In this final section, we'll discuss strategies for practicing forgiveness and letting go.

Acknowledge the Hurt: Recognize and validate the pain and hurt you've experienced as a result of fatherlessness. By acknowledging these emotions, you create space for healing and forgiveness.

Understand the Context: Recognize that your father's absence was likely the result of his own pain, struggles, or limitations. Understanding this context can help you cultivate empathy and forgiveness.

Release the Anger: Find healthy ways to release your anger and resentment, whether through journaling, physical activity, or creative expression. By letting go of these emotions, you'll create space for forgiveness and healing.

Practice Forgiveness: Actively practice forgiveness, both for your father and for yourself. Remember that forgiveness is a journey, not a destination, and may require ongoing effort and self-compassion.

Chapter 4: Healing from the Trauma of Fatherlessness

From Pain to Power

As we conclude this chapter, remember that healing from the trauma of fatherlessness is a lifelong journey filled with growth, resilience, and self-discovery. By acknowledging the effects of fatherlessness, embracing strategies for healing and growth, building a support network, and ultimately practicing forgiveness and letting go of the past, you can emerge stronger, wiser, and more resilient than ever before.

"Being a father is a full-time job. It requires a lot of sacrifice, but it's all worth it for the love and joy my children bring me." Lil Baby

Name: _____   Date: _____

Chapter 4 Quiz
Lets see what you learned in chapter #4

1. Growing up without a father figure can impact your sense of _____, leading to feelings of inadequacy or a lack of confidence

   _____

2. In order to heal and grow, you must first identify and acknowledge the _____ of fatherlessness

   _____

3. Establish healthy _____ in your relationships, ensuring that you prioritize your own well-being and emotional safety.

   _____

4. Therapy offers a safe and _____ space for you to explore your emotions, experiences, and challenges without fear of judgment or repercussions.

   _____

5. Practice _____, both for your father and for yourself.

   _____

6. Which of the following is NOT a strategy for healing and personal growth?

   a) Self-reflection
   b) Blaming others
   c) Embrace vulnerability
   d) Set boundaries

Name: _____ Date: _____

Chapter 4 Quiz
Lets see what you learned in chapter #4

7. What can therapists and counselors provide to help you navigate your healing process?
   a) Unbiased perspective
   b) Expertise
   c) Safe space
   d) All of the above

Journal Prompts
Reflect on the emotional impact of fatherlessness in your life. How has it affected your relationships, self-identity, and coping mechanisms?

Describe a situation in which you practiced vulnerability with someone. How did it impact your relationship with that person and your healing journey?

Write about a time when you had to set boundaries in a relationship. How did it affect your well-being and emotional safety?

Personal Reflection
Think about one or two people you could reach out to as you begin building your support network. What qualities do they possess that make them good candidates for offering guidance, encouragement, and understanding during your healing journey?

Chapter #5 Personal Growth and Becoming the Man You Were Meant to Be

"As a father, you have to be present and engaged in your children's lives. You have to listen to them, support them, and guide them." Jason Wilson

Chapter 5: Personal Growth and Becoming the Man You Were Meant to Be

Unleashing Your Inner Hero

Picture a caterpillar, slowly and methodically making its way through life, inching along and doing its best to survive. Then, one day, it undergoes a miraculous transformation and emerges as a breathtaking butterfly, full of color, grace, and newfound freedom. This metaphorical journey from caterpillar to butterfly is not unlike the path of personal growth and development, as we strive to transform ourselves and become the men we were meant to be.

In this chapter, we'll explore practical strategies for personal growth, focusing on building self-awareness, setting goals, and embracing vulnerability as a father. So, strap on your metaphorical wings, and let's take flight on this journey of self-discovery and transformation.

Chapter 5: Personal Growth and Becoming the Man You Were Meant to Be

Identifying and Developing Personal Values and Beliefs

The foundation of personal growth lies in understanding and embracing your values and beliefs. In this section, we'll delve into the process of identifying and developing your personal values, providing a compass to guide your actions and decisions.

Self-Reflection: Engage in regular self-reflection, examining your thoughts, feelings, and experiences to identify the values and beliefs that drive you. Consider using journaling, meditation, or other introspective practices to aid in this process.

Values Exploration: Create a list of values that resonate with you, and then narrow it down to your top 5-10 core values. These values will serve as the foundation for your personal growth and decision-making.

Align Your Actions: Once you've identified your core values, evaluate your current actions and decisions to ensure they align with these guiding principles. If you find discrepancies, consider how you can adjust your behaviors to better reflect your values.

Embrace Growth: Recognize that your values and beliefs may evolve over time as you grow and learn. Be open to this growth, and be willing to reassess your values as needed.

Chapter 5: Personal Growth and Becoming the Man You Were Meant to Be

Developing Self-Awareness and Emotional Intelligence

Emotional intelligence and self-awareness are critical components of personal growth, enabling you to better understand and navigate your emotions and those of others. In this section, we'll explore strategies for cultivating emotional intelligence and self-awareness.

1. Mindfulness: Practice mindfulness techniques such as meditation, deep breathing, or body scans to help you become more attuned to your emotions and internal experiences.

Emotional Vocabulary: Expand your emotional vocabulary, learning to identify and label your emotions with greater accuracy and nuance. This will enable you to better understand and process your feelings.

Empathy: Develop empathy by actively listening to others, validating their emotions, and striving to understand their experiences. This will not only improve your relationships but also enhance your emotional intelligence.

Self-Regulation: Learn to regulate your emotions through healthy coping strategies, such as exercise, journaling, or engaging in creative outlets. This will help you maintain emotional balance and resilience in the face of adversity.

Chapter 5: Personal Growth and Becoming the Man You Were Meant to Be

Setting and Achieving Personal and Professional Goals

Goal-setting is a powerful tool for personal growth, providing direction, motivation, and a sense of accomplishment. In this section, we'll discuss strategies for setting and achieving meaningful personal and professional goals.

SMART Goals: Embrace the SMART goal-setting framework, ensuring that your goals are Specific, Measurable, Achievable, Relevant, and Time-bound. This will increase your chances of success and help you maintain focus and motivation.

Break It Down: Break your larger goals into smaller, manageable steps, and create a detailed action plan for achieving them. This will help you maintain momentum and track your progress more easily.

Accountability Partners: Enlist the help of an accountability partner, such as a friend, family member, or coach, who can provide support, encouragement, and guidance as you work towards your goals. Sharing your goals with someone else can increase your motivation and commitment.

Celebrate Success: Celebrate your successes, both big and small, as you achieve your goals. Acknowledging your accomplishments will help boost your confidence and motivation, propelling you forward on your journey of personal growth.

Chapter 5: Personal Growth and Becoming the Man You Were Meant to Be

Embracing Vulnerability and Authenticity

Vulnerability and authenticity are essential ingredients for personal growth, allowing you to connect deeply with others and live a life true to yourself. In this section, we'll explore strategies for embracing vulnerability and cultivating authenticity.

Drop the Mask: Let go of the need to project a perfect image, and allow yourself to be seen and loved for who you truly are. By embracing your imperfections, you'll create space for genuine connection and self-acceptance.

Share Your Story: Open up about your experiences, emotions, and challenges, sharing your story with others. This will not only deepen your relationships but also help you embrace your own vulnerability and authenticity.

Practice Courage: Be willing to take risks, face your fears, and step outside your comfort zone. By doing so, you'll build courage and resilience, allowing you to embrace vulnerability with greater ease.

Cultivate Self-Compassion: Treat yourself with kindness and understanding, recognizing that vulnerability and authenticity require ongoing effort and self-compassion.

Chapter 5: Personal Growth and Becoming the Man You Were Meant to Be

Building Resilience and Adapting to Change

Life is filled with change and adversity, and the ability to adapt and bounce back from these challenges is crucial for personal growth. In this section, we'll discuss strategies for building resilience and embracing change.

Embrace Change: Adopt a growth mindset, viewing change and adversity as opportunities for learning and growth. By embracing change, you'll develop the flexibility and resilience needed to thrive in an ever-evolving world.

Learn from Failure: Rather than viewing failure as a setback, see it as a valuable learning experience. Analyze your failures to identify areas for growth, and use this information to propel yourself forward.

Cultivate a Support Network: Surround yourself with a strong support network of friends, family, and mentors who can provide encouragement, guidance, and a shoulder to lean on during challenging times.

Practice Self-Care: Prioritize self-care, ensuring that you are nurturing your physical, emotional, and mental well-being. By taking care of yourself, you'll be better equipped to handle life's challenges and continue on your path of personal growth.

Chapter 5: Personal Growth and Becoming the Man You Were Meant to Be

The Journey of a Lifetime

As we wrap up this chapter, remember that personal growth is an ongoing, lifelong journey. It is a process of continual learning, self-discovery, and transformation as you strive to become the man you were meant to be. By identifying and developing your values and beliefs, cultivating self-awareness and emotional intelligence, setting and achieving goals, embracing vulnerability and authenticity, and building resilience in the face of change, you'll not only grow as a father but also as a man.

So, as you embark on this transformative journey, keep in mind the words of the ancient Chinese philosopher Lao Tzu: "A journey of a thousand miles begins with a single step." Take that first step today, and embrace the incredible adventure of personal growth that lies ahead.

"Fatherhood is not a solo journey. You need to build a support network of other fathers who can help you on this journey."
Jason Wilson

Name: _____   Date: _____

Chapter 5 Quiz
Lets see what you learned in chapter #5

1. The foundation of personal growth lies in understanding and embracing your _____ and _____.

   _____

2. Which of the following is NOT a component of emotional intelligence?

   a. Mindfulness
   b. Emotional Vocabulary
   c. Empathy
   d. Perfectionism

   _____

3. Embrace the _____ goal-setting framework, which stands for Specific, Measurable, Achievable, Relevant, and Time-bound.

   _____

4. Which of the following is NOT a strategy for building resilience and adapting to change?

   a. Embrace change
   b. Learn from failure
   c. Avoid challenges
   d. Cultivate a support network

   _____

Name: _____   Date: _____

Chapter 5 Quiz
Lets see what you learned in chapter #5

5. Journaling Prompt:
   Reflect on a recent situation in which you felt vulnerable. How did you handle it? What could you have done differently to embrace vulnerability and authenticity in that moment?

---

6. Journaling Prompt:
   What is one small step you can take today to embark on your journey of personal growth? Write down your commitment and reflect on how this step will contribute to your overall growth and development.

Chapter #6 Learning from Experts and Other Fatherless Fathers

> "Fatherhood is about teaching your children how to face the world with confidence, courage, and integrity." Jordan Peterson

Chapter 6: Learning from Experts and Other Fatherless Fathers

The Power of Shared Wisdom

There is an ancient African proverb that says, "If you want to go fast, go alone. If you want to go far, go together." This wisdom holds true in the journey of fatherhood, especially for fatherless fathers seeking to break the cycle and create a brighter future for their children. By connecting with experts and other fatherless fathers, you can glean valuable insights, support, and camaraderie that will enrich and inform your fatherhood journey.

In this chapter, we will explore the benefits of learning from others' experiences and perspectives, focusing on the invaluable contributions of experts and fellow fatherless fathers. So, let's dive in and discover the power of shared wisdom in charting the path forward.

Chapter 6: Learning from Experts and Other Fatherless Fathers

The Benefits of Expert Insights and Experiences

The insights and experiences of experts in fields such as psychology, family therapy, and personal growth can provide valuable guidance and inspiration for fatherless fathers. In this section, we will discuss the benefits of tapping into this wealth of knowledge.

Evidence-Based Strategies: By learning from experts, you gain access to evidence-based strategies and techniques that have been proven effective in addressing the challenges faced by fatherless fathers. These research-backed approaches can increase your chances of success in your fatherhood journey.

Perspective Shifts: Engaging with expert insights can help you develop new perspectives on fatherlessness, allowing you to reframe your experiences and challenges in more constructive and empowering ways.

Personalized Advice: Experts can provide tailored advice based on your unique circumstances, helping you navigate the complexities of fatherhood with greater clarity and confidence.

Emotional Support: Connecting with experts who understand the emotional and psychological impact of fatherlessness can provide much-needed support and validation, helping you feel less alone in your journey.

Chapter 6: Learning from Experts and Other Fatherless Fathers

Understanding Different Perspectives on Fatherlessness

Fatherlessness is a complex and multifaceted issue that affects individuals in diverse ways. In this section, we will discuss the importance of understanding different perspectives on fatherlessness, highlighting the value of empathy and open-mindedness.

Empathy: By learning from the experiences of others who have navigated fatherlessness, you can develop a deeper sense of empathy for their struggles and triumphs, fostering a sense of connection and mutual support.

Open-Mindedness: Listening to diverse perspectives on fatherlessness can help you cultivate an open mind, allowing you to appreciate the unique challenges and opportunities that others face in their fatherhood journeys.

Challenging Assumptions: Encountering different perspectives can challenge your assumptions about fatherlessness, inspiring you to reevaluate and refine your understanding of this complex issue.

Expanding Your Toolbox: As you learn from others' experiences and insights, you will acquire new tools and strategies for addressing fatherlessness in your own life, broadening your repertoire of coping mechanisms and resources.

Chapter 6: Learning from Experts and Other Fatherless Fathers

Networking and Building Connections within the Fatherless Fathers Community

Fostering connections with other fatherless fathers can provide a powerful sense of community and belonging. In this section, we will explore the benefits of networking and building connections within the fatherless fathers community.

Shared Understanding: Connecting with other fatherless fathers allows you to engage with individuals who share a deep understanding of your experiences, providing a sense of validation and camaraderie.

Emotional Support: Building a support network of fellow fatherless fathers can offer invaluable emotional support, as you navigate the challenges of fatherhood together.

Practical Advice: Your fellow fatherless fathers can offer practical advice and insights based on their own experiences, providing valuable guidance and inspiration for your fatherhood journey.

Accountability and Motivation: By connecting with others who share your goals and values, you can foster a sense of accountability and motivation, helping you stay on track in your personal growth and fatherhood journey.

Chapter 6: Learning from Experts and Other Fatherless Fathers

Applying Lessons Learned to Your Own Fatherhood Journey

With a wealth of insights and experiences at your fingertips, the final step is to apply these lessons to your own fatherhood journey. In this section, we will discuss strategies for integrating the wisdom you've gained from experts and fellow fatherless fathers.

Reflect and Evaluate: Take time to reflect on the insights and experiences you've encountered, evaluating which strategies and perspectives resonate most deeply with your own situation and goals.

Experiment and Adapt: Be willing to experiment with different approaches and techniques, adapting them to fit your unique circumstances and needs. Remember that personal growth and fatherhood are ongoing journeys, and there is always room for growth and improvement.

Set Realistic Goals: As you learn from others' experiences and insights, use this knowledge to set realistic and achievable goals for yourself. By breaking down your objectives into manageable steps, you'll be better equipped to make meaningful progress in your fatherhood journey

Chapter 6: Learning from Experts and Other Fatherless Fathers

Stay Connected: Maintain your connections with experts and fellow fatherless fathers, continually seeking out new perspectives and insights. As you grow and evolve in your fatherhood journey, staying connected with others who share your experiences can provide ongoing support and encouragement.

The Strength of Shared Wisdom

As we conclude this chapter, remember that you are not alone in your journey as a fatherless father. By connecting with experts and other fatherless fathers, you can access a wealth of shared wisdom and support, empowering you to become the best father, partner, and man you can be.

So, reach out, listen, and learn from the experiences and insights of others. Embrace the power of shared wisdom, and let it guide you on your path to breaking the cycle of fatherlessness and creating a brighter future for yourself and your family. In the words of the poet John Donne, "No man is an island, entire of itself; every man is a piece of the continent, a part of the main." Together, we can chart the path forward and help one another rise above the challenges of fatherlessness, forging a legacy of love, strength, and resilience for future generations.

"Being a father is about leading by example. You have to model the behavior you want your children to emulate." Tony Robbins

Name: _____   Date: _____

Chapter 6 Quiz

Lets see what you learned in chapter #6

1. By learning from experts, fatherless fathers can access _____-based strategies and techniques.

   _____

2. Which of the following is NOT a benefit of understanding different perspectives on fatherlessness?

   a. Empathy
   b. Open-mindedness
   c. Challenging assumptions
   d. Relying on stereotypes

   _____

3. As you learn from others' experiences and insights, use this knowledge to set _____ and _____ goals for yourself.

   _____

4. Journaling Prompt:
   Reflect on any connections you have made with other fatherless fathers or experts. How have these connections impacted your fatherhood journey? If you haven't made any connections yet, what steps can you take to build a support network?

   _____

Name: _____   Date: _____

Chapter 6 Quiz
Lets see what you learned in chapter #6

5. Journaling Prompt:
   Identify one valuable lesson or insight you have gained from an expert or another fatherless father. How can you apply this lesson to your own fatherhood journey? Write down specific steps you can take to integrate this wisdom into your life.

Chapter #7 Being a Role Model for Your Children and Future Generations

"To be a good father and mother requires that the parents defer many of their own needs and desires in favor of the needs of their children. As a consequence of this sacrifice, conscientious parents develop a nobility of character and learn to put into practice the selfless truths taught by the Savior Himself." - James E. Faust

Chapter 7: Being a Role Model for Your Children and Future Generations

The Enduring Impact of Fatherhood

Your role as a father has a lasting impact on your children and future generations. Like a stone tossed into a pond, the ripple effect of your actions and choices as a father can reverberate through time, shaping the lives of those who come after you. In this chapter, we will discuss the importance of being a positive role model and strategies for instilling values and principles in your children, with an eye toward fostering a lasting legacy of love, strength, and resilience.

Chapter 7: Being a Role Model for Your Children and Future Generations

The Importance of Being a Positive Role Model

As a father, you have the unique privilege and responsibility of serving as a role model for your children. In this section, we will explore the profound impact that your example can have on their lives and the lives of future generations.

Shaping Identity: Your children look to you as they develop their own sense of identity, drawing upon your example as they forge their beliefs, values, and sense of self.

Emotional Well-Being: By modeling healthy emotional expression and self-awareness, you can help your children develop emotional intelligence, resilience, and empathy, equipping them to navigate life's challenges with grace and confidence.

Moral Compass: As a father, you have the opportunity to instill a strong moral compass in your children, guiding them in making wise and compassionate choices throughout their lives.

Lifelong Impact: The lessons your children learn from your example will continue to shape their lives long after they leave the nest, influencing their relationships, careers, and personal growth for years to come.

Chapter 7: Being a Role Model for Your Children and Future Generations

Instilling Values and Principles in Your Children

The values and principles you instill in your children will serve as the foundation for their character, guiding them through life's challenges and opportunities. In this section, we will discuss strategies for fostering a strong moral compass and a sense of personal responsibility in your children.

Be Intentional: Take the time to consider the values and principles you wish to instill in your children, creating a clear and consistent framework for their moral development.

Model the Way: Strive to embody the values and principles you wish to teach your children, demonstrating through your actions and choices the importance of living with integrity, compassion, and purpose.

Engage in Conversation: Encourage open and honest discussions about values and principles with your children, fostering a sense of curiosity and inquiry as they develop their own moral compass.

Provide Guidance: Offer gentle guidance and support as your children navigate the complexities of life, helping them to learn from their mistakes and grow in wisdom and understanding.

Chapter 7: Being a Role Model for Your Children and Future Generations

I Encouraging and Supporting Your Children's Dreams and Aspirations

As a father, you play a pivotal role in helping your children discover and pursue their dreams and aspirations. In this section, we will explore strategies for nurturing your children's talents and interests, fostering a sense of purpose and passion in their lives.

Listen and Observe: Pay close attention to your children's interests, passions, and talents, seeking to understand and appreciate their unique gifts and dreams.

Encourage Exploration: Provide opportunities for your children to explore their interests and passions, fostering a sense of curiosity, creativity, and self-discovery.

Offer Support: Be a source of unwavering support and encouragement as your children pursue their dreams, offering guidance, resources, and a listening ear along the way.

Celebrate Success: Acknowledge and celebrate your children's achievements and milestones, helping them to recognize their progress and build a sense of self-confidence and accomplishment.

Chapter 7: Being a Role Model for Your Children and Future Generations

Promoting Healthy Relationships and Communication within the Family

Healthy relationships and open communication are the cornerstones of a strong and resilient family. In this section, we will discuss strategies for promoting harmony and understanding within your family, fostering a sense of connection and belonging for all.

Model Respectful Communication: Set the tone for healthy communication within your family by modeling active listening, empathy, and respect in your interactions with your partner and children.

Encourage Open Dialogue: Create a safe space for your children to express their thoughts, feelings, and concerns, fostering an atmosphere of trust and understanding within your family.

Teach Conflict Resolution Skills: Equip your children with the tools they need to navigate disagreements and conflicts, helping them to build strong, lasting relationships throughout their lives.

Prioritize Family Time: Make time for regular family activities and rituals, reinforcing the importance of connection and unity within your family.

Chapter 7: Being a Role Model for Your Children and Future Generations

Leaving a Legacy for Future Generations

As a father, you have the opportunity to leave a lasting legacy for your children and future generations. In this final section, we will explore strategies for creating a legacy of love, strength, and resilience that can ripple through time.

Reflect on Your Impact: Take time to consider the lasting impact of your actions and choices, recognizing the profound influence you have on your children's lives and the lives of those who come after them.

Share Your Wisdom: Pass down the lessons you've learned through your own experiences and personal growth, equipping your children with the wisdom and insight they need to navigate life's challenges and opportunities.

Foster a Sense of Purpose: Help your children discover and embrace their unique purpose in life, encouraging them to pursue their passions and make a positive impact on the world around them.

Embrace Your Imperfections: Recognize that you, too, are a work in progress, striving to grow and learn as a father, partner, and man. By embracing your imperfections and demonstrating resilience in the face of adversity, you can inspire your children to do the same.

Chapter 7: Being a Role Model for Your Children and Future Generations

The Ripple Effect of Fatherhood

As we conclude this chapter, remember that your role as a father has a lasting impact on your children and future generations. By embracing your responsibility as a role model, instilling values and principles in your children, and fostering a strong sense of connection and belonging within your family, you can create a legacy that ripples through time, shaping the lives of those who come after you.

So, let your actions and choices serve as a beacon of hope and inspiration for your children and future generations, illuminating the path to a brighter, more compassionate, and resilient world. And remember the words of American author and poet Maya Angelou: "People will forget what you said, people will forget what you did, but people will never forget how you made them feel." Let the legacy of your fatherhood journey be one of love, strength, and resilience, casting a ripple effect that echoes through the generations to come.

"The role of the father is to make sure that the children don't do anything that will prevent them from developing into useful, competent, honest, and self-reliant adults." Jordan Peterson

Name: _____   Date: _____

Chapter 7 Quiz

Lets see what you learned in chapter #7

1. As a father, you have the unique privilege and responsibility of serving as a _____ for your children.

   _____

2. Which of the following is NOT a strategy for fostering a strong moral compass in your children?

   a. Be intentional
   b. Model the way
   c. Engage in conversation
   d. Ignore their mistakes

   _____

3. _____ and open communication are the cornerstones of a strong and resilient family.

   _____

4. Journaling Prompt:
   Reflect on a time when your child expressed a dream or aspiration. How did you respond? What steps can you take to provide better support and encouragement for their dreams in the future?

   _____

Name: _____ Date: _____

Chapter 7 Quiz
Lets see what you learned in chapter #7

5. Journaling Prompt:
   Consider the legacy you want to leave for your children and future generations. What values, principles, or life lessons do you hope to pass down? How can you actively work towards instilling these in your children?

Chapter #8 Embracing Imperfection and Growth as a Fatherless Father

"The greatest legacy one can pass on to one's children and grandchildren is not money or other material things accumulated in one's life, but rather a legacy of character and faith." - Billy Graham

Chapter 8: Embracing Imperfection and Growth as a Fatherless Father

The Path Toward Healing and Growth

Throughout this book, we have explored strategies for overcoming fatherlessness, building strong relationships with our children and partners, and nurturing personal growth. As we reach the conclusion of our journey together, it is important to recognize that this is not the end, but merely the beginning of a lifelong process of self-discovery, healing, and growth as a father, partner, and man.

In this final chapter, we will reflect on the key lessons learned throughout the book, providing a roadmap for continued growth and development as a fatherless father. Through wit, humor, and honest reflection, we will celebrate the progress made thus far and look ahead to the journey that lies before us, embracing our imperfections and striving to become the best version of ourselves for the sake of our children, partners, and communities.

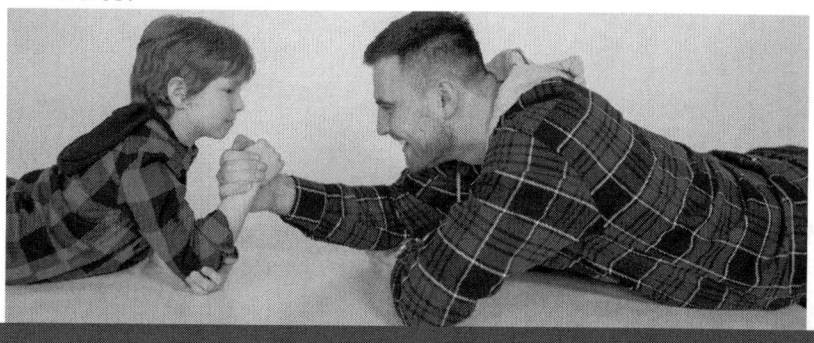

Chapter 8: Embracing Imperfection and Growth as a Fatherless Father

The Journey Thus Far: Key Lessons and Insights

As we look back on our journey together, let us pause to reflect on the key lessons and insights gained throughout the book:

The Power of Connection: The importance of building strong, nurturing relationships with our children, partners, and support networks, fostering a sense of belonging and resilience in the face of adversity.

The Art of Communication: The crucial role of effective communication in promoting understanding, empathy, and emotional intelligence within our families and communities.

The Courage to Heal: The journey of healing from the trauma of fatherlessness, embracing vulnerability, forgiveness, and self-compassion as we strive to break the cycle and create a brighter future for ourselves and our children.

The Quest for Growth: The pursuit of personal growth and self-awareness as we strive to become the men we were meant to be, embracing our imperfections and learning from our experiences.

The Ripple Effect: The enduring impact of our actions and choices as fathers, serving as role models for our children and future generations, and shaping the world around us for the better.

Chapter 8: Embracing Imperfection and Growth as a Fatherless Father

Embracing Imperfection and Growth

As fatherless fathers, it is essential that we embrace our imperfections and strive for growth, recognizing that we are works in progress, continually evolving and learning on our journey through fatherhood.

The Power of Humility: Recognizing our limitations and acknowledging our mistakes, fostering a spirit of humility and openness to growth and change.

The Art of Self-Compassion: Cultivating self-compassion and self-care, nurturing our emotional well-being, and promoting resilience in the face of adversity.

The Courage to Ask for Help: Seeking support and guidance from others when needed, fostering a sense of connection and community as we navigate the challenges of fatherhood.

The Quest for Balance: Striving for balance in our personal and professional lives, nurturing our relationships, and prioritizing our physical, emotional, and spiritual well-being.

Chapter 8: Embracing Imperfection and Growth as a Fatherless Father

The Road Ahead: Continuing the Journey

As we look to the future, let us consider the road ahead, embracing the opportunities and challenges that lie before us as we continue our journey through fatherhood.

The Power of Persistence: Staying the course, even when the path is difficult or uncertain, recognizing the importance of perseverance and resilience in the face of adversity.

The Art of Adaptation: Embracing change and uncertainty, learning to adapt and grow in response to the evolving needs of our families and communities.

The Courage to Dream: Pursuing our dreams and aspirations, both as individuals and as fathers, inspiring our children to do the same.

The Quest for Legacy: Striving to leave a lasting legacy of love, strength, and resilience for our children and future generations, casting a ripple effect that echoes through the generations to come.

Chapter 8: Embracing Imperfection and Growth as a Fatherless Father

A Call to Action: Embracing Your Fatherhood Journey

As we conclude our time together, let us take a moment to reflect on our journey and consider the call to action that lies before us. As fatherless fathers, we have the unique opportunity and responsibility to rise above our past, break the cycle of fatherlessness, and create a brighter future for ourselves, our children, and our communities.

Embrace the Journey: Recognize that your fatherhood journey is a lifelong process of growth, learning, and self-discovery. Embrace the challenges, triumphs, and lessons along the way.

Commit to Growth: Dedicate yourself to personal and professional growth, continually striving to become the best version of yourself for the benefit of your family and community.

Foster Connection: Cultivate deep, meaningful connections with your children, partner, and support network, recognizing that relationships are the foundation of a happy, healthy, and fulfilling life.

Serve as a Role Model: Be a beacon of hope and inspiration for your children and future generations, embodying the values and principles that you wish to instill in them.

Chapter 8: Embracing Imperfection and Growth as a Fatherless Father

A Lifelong Journey of Growth and Love

As we bid farewell, remember that our journey together is merely the beginning of a lifelong adventure of growth, healing, and self-discovery. Embrace the challenges, triumphs, and lessons that lie ahead, and let the wisdom and insights gained throughout this book serve as a compass to guide you on your path.

As you continue your fatherhood journey, let us remember the words of author and motivational speaker, John C. Maxwell: "Growth is the great separator between those who succeed and those who do not. When I see a person beginning to separate themselves from the pack, it's almost always due to personal growth."

So, let your journey through fatherhood be a testament to the power of growth, resilience, and love, casting a ripple effect that touches the lives of your children, your partner, your community, and the generations to come. And as you embrace your role as a fatherless father, remember that you are not alone. Together, we can break the cycle of fatherlessness, heal our hearts, and create a brighter, more compassionate, and resilient world for all.

"Fatherhood is not a role that you can ever retire from. It's a lifelong commitment to your children and your family." Jordan Peterson

Name: _____ Date: _____

Chapter 8 Quiz

Lets see what you learned in chapter #8

1. The journey of healing from the trauma of fatherlessness includes embracing vulnerability, forgiveness, and _____ as we strive to break the cycle and create a brighter future for ourselves and our children.

   _____

2. Which of the following is NOT a key aspect of embracing imperfection and growth as a fatherless father?

   a. The Power of Humility
   b. The Art of Self-Compassion
   c. The Courage to Ask for Help
   d. The Importance of Perfectionism

   _____

3. As a fatherless father, you have the unique opportunity and responsibility to rise above your past, break the cycle of _____, and create a brighter future for yourself, your children, and your communities.

   _____

4. Journaling Prompt:
   Reflect on your personal journey as a fatherless father so far. What challenges have you faced, and what triumphs have you experienced? How can you use these experiences to guide your continued growth as a father, partner, and man?

   _____

AFFIRMATIONS FOR FATHERLESS FATHERS:

I am capable of being a great father, despite not having had a father figure in my life.

My experiences growing up without a father have given me unique insights and strengths as a parent.

I am worthy of love and respect, both from myself and from my children.

I have the power to break the cycle of fatherlessness and provide a positive role model for my children.

I am strong and resilient, and I can overcome any challenges that come my way.

I am doing the best I can as a father, and that is enough.

I am grateful for the opportunity to be a father and to provide love and support to my children.

AFFIRMATIONS FOR FATHERLESS FATHERS:

I am constantly learning and growing as a parent, and I am open to new experiences and perspectives.

I trust my instincts as a parent and have faith in my ability to make the best decisions for my children.

I am proud of myself for being a loving and supportive father to my children, despite the challenges I have faced.

Fatherhood Communication Checklist

This checklist is designed to help fathers improve their communication skills with their children. Whether you are looking to build stronger relationships with your children or want to learn how to communicate more effectively, this checklist is a great place to start.

Listen actively and empathetically

When your child is speaking, actively listen and show that you understand what they are saying. This can involve asking clarifying questions or reflecting back on what they have said.

Avoid criticism and focus on constructive feedback

Criticism can be hurtful and may not lead to positive change. Instead, try to provide feedback in a constructive way that focuses on finding solutions.
Example: "I noticed that you didn't finish your homework. Is there anything I can do to help you?"

Be present and attentive during conversations

Show your child that you value their thoughts and feelings by giving them your full attention during conversations.
Example: Put down your phone or turn off the TV when your child is talking to you.

Practice patience and understanding

Communication can be difficult at times, but being patient and understanding can help to create a safe and supportive environment for your child to express themselves.
Example: Take a deep breath and try to remain calm when your child is upset or emotional.

Encourage open and honest communication

Encourage your child to express themselves and create an open and honest dialogue between you both.
Example: "I want you to know that you can always come to me with anything. I will always be here to listen."

Use positive reinforcement and praise

Celebrate your child's achievements and positive behaviors with praise and positive reinforcement.
Example: "I am so proud of you for getting an A on your test!"

Fatherhood Communication Checklist

This checklist is designed to help fathers improve their communication skills with their children. Whether you are looking to build stronger relationships with your children or want to learn how to communicate more effectively, this checklist is a great place to start.

Recognize and address your own emotions before communicating

Before engaging in communication with your child, take a moment to recognize and address any emotions or feelings that may interfere with effective communication. Example: Take a few deep breaths and center yourself before talking to your child about a difficult topic.

Stay calm and avoid reacting impulsively

SResponding in the heat of the moment can sometimes lead to negative communication. Take a step back and respond in a calm and thoughtful manner.
Example: "I need a moment to think about what you just said. Let's talk about this more later."

Show respect and consideration for your child's feelings and opinions

Let your child know that you respect their feelings and opinions, even if you may not always agree with them.
Example: "I understand that you may not want to go to bed right now, but it's important for your health and well-being. Let's work together to find a compromise."

30 Day Challenge
CHECKLIST

Day 1: Introduce yourself and why you're passionate about helping fathers overcome fatherlessness. Use the hashtag #ImperfectFathersGuideChallenge

Day 2: Share a picture of your own father and share one positive memory you have with him.

Day 3: Share a quote or passage from "Dad By Choice" that resonated with you and explain why.

Day 4: Share a picture or video of a moment you had with your own child(ren) that made you proud to be their father.

Day 5: Post a video sharing one piece of advice from "Dad By Choice" that has helped you in your own journey as a father.

Day 6: Share a picture or video of a father figure in your life who has had a positive impact on you.

Day 7: Post a blog or video about a challenge you faced as a father and how you overcame it.

Day 8: Share a quote or passage from "Dad By Choice" that you think is important for all fathers to remember

Day 9: Share a picture or video of a father/child activity that you enjoy doing together.

Day 10: Post a video about your own experience growing up without a father and how it has affected your journey as a dad.

30 Day Challenge
CHECKLIST

Day 11: Share a story about a time you made a mistake as a father and what you learned from it.

Day 12: Share a picture or video of a father in your life who has shown strength and resilience in the face of adversity

Day 13: Share a quote or passage from "Dad By Choice" that you found particularly inspiring

Day 14: Post a blog or video about a successful moment you've had as a father and what you learned from it.

Day 15: Share a picture or video of a father figure in your life who has taught you an important lesson.

Day 16: Post a video sharing one piece of advice you would give to a new father.

Day 17: Share a quote or passage from "Dad By Choice" that challenges you to be a better father.

Day 18: Share a picture or video of a father/child moment that made you laugh.

Day 19: Post a blog or video about a time you had to apologize to your child and what you learned from the experience.

Day 20: Share a picture or video of a father figure who has taught you the value of hard work.

30 Day Challenge
CHECKLIST

Day 21: Post a video about how you balance work and family life.

Day 22: Share a quote or passage from "Dad By Choice" that speaks to the importance of communication in fatherhood

Day 23: Share a picture or video of a father/child moment that made you feel grateful.

Day 24: Post a blog or video about a time you had to make a tough decision as a father and how you came to that decision.

Day 25: Share a picture or video of a father figure who has shown you the importance of self-care.

Day 26: Share a quote or passage from "Dad By Choice" that encourages you to be present in your child's life.

Day 27: Post a video about how you incorporate family traditions into your life as a father.

Day 28: Share a picture or video of a father/child moment that taught you an important lesson.

Day 29: Post a blog or video about a time you had to be vulnerable as a father and what you learned from it.

Day 30: Share a final post reflecting on your 30-day journey and what you have learned about yourself and your journey as a father

THE IMPERFECT GENTLEMEN'S OUTLET

Are you a fatherless father struggling to find balance in your role as a dad? Do you feel like you could use some support and guidance from other men who have been there before?

If so, we invite you to join our coaching program, The Imperfect Gentlemen's Outlet. Our group is a safe and supportive space for men to come together, share their experiences, and learn from one another.

Led by experienced coaches, our program focuses on building better relationships with your kids, improving communication with your partner, and finding fulfillment in your role as a father figure. Don't let the challenges of being a dad by choice overwhelm you. Join our community of imperfect gentlemen and start thriving in your role as a father figure. Sign up now and discover the power of support, accountability, and brotherhood.

SUBSCRIBE AT

?